Kathleen

Kathleen

by Amanda Jones
illustrated by Kathleen Woodland

Bridge House

British Library Cataloguing in Publication Data

A Record of this Publication is available from the British Library

ISBN 978-1-914199-60-8

This edition published 2024 by Bridge House Publishing
Manchester, England

Dedicated to Mum

Contents

Introduction

Written with healing at heart and love learned through care, this book is about Kathleen, my mum. I want to wrap you in the possibility that life reaches out and holds you in your light.

9

They Said

They said the pain was all in her head. She had struggled since being a tiny baby due to a mishap which damaged her bowel. But, no-one would listen.

Moving away and renting her own flat in Blackpool in the 1960s gave her time to think in her late teens. Somehow she found the strength to approach the hospital.

They sent her to the psychiatric hospital after tests were 'fine'.

And so, she experienced electric shock treatment. The sort once used to 'cure' homosexuality. The treatment was approved for stimulating seizures to get rid of depression. All of her pain was blamed on mental illness.

Subjected to intensive electric shocks two to three times a week and kept in the secure mental health unit she saw terrible things. People were severely mentally ill here and she forced herself to think she was imagining her pain.

Tightly pressed on either side of her head she dreaded the next session, and the next and the next. She was awake throughout and felt the shocks passing through her, convulsing her body.

Then she was discharged, back into the community, no explanation, still in pain.

Strong, loving lady.

How did she get through? How did she survive so long in pain?

Dark

She lay on the couch. For days there had been so many visits to the loo and a thirst which ravaged her relentlessly. Just a virus, nothing to worry about, the doctor said. Yet here she was, unable to move, exhausted.

So it was a huge relief when the dark came. Sweeping over her it seemed to take on a life of its own. It was a strangeness. Lying there with nothing but darkness. In limbo. Between worlds.

It was 1959, she was ten years old. The ambulance rushed her into hospital, but she was still in the dark. Nothing.

Only when the insulin came did she awaken. Diabetic Ketoacidosis they said. Nearly died. A diabetic coma. They taught her how to inject using big, metal syringes and to test her sugar levels in her urine. And there was still the pain.

It is strange how it all became normal so quickly.

This was the beginning of a journey. Very high blood sugar at the start when her pancreas failed to produce insulin meant a very long, chronic illness ahead.

What would she do? How did she manage? What were her dreams?

Such Need

The desire and instinct had always been there. An urge and demand that wouldn't let go. She found her man and married to allow the beginnings.

Sex was painful. Diabetes had put a hold on puberty long ago and she was left with scanty if non-existent periods. Tilted positions to encourage conception were suggested and followed. This was 1976 and before IVF, yet not too far from the first test-tube baby in 1978.

She wanted a baby above all else. It was a motherly obsession and led to the fertility clinic.

Treatment consisted of hormones beyond hormones. The oestrogen rippled through her body and over-stimulated her ovaries. But, then in 1978 she fell pregnant.

Diabetes and pregnancy didn't mix. For many months she stayed in hospital with high blood pressure and on bed rest. The clinical sterility and monitoring a way of being, she saw little of her outside life. They held on and on, trying to prolong delivery.

Eight weeks before the due date baby was in danger and a caesarean could be put off no longer. Whilst under she felt the thuds of a defibrillator and saw a bright, white light. People huddled round and said, 'it's not your time yet,' until she landed with a thump back into reality. Blueness and puffiness presented in her baby. She was a 'miracle baby' declared the doctors as she was rushed off to intensive care. But she was to have no more and they sterilised her to prevent this.

All too quickly she was home with her little one.

Months of exhaustion in hospital led to fainting and overwhelming tiredness at home. Her sugar levels were all over the place and her body tried to adjust. No breast milk was willing and life became 'looking after baby' as her little girl cried and cried. She didn't want to keep her milk down either.

So, she was accused of being lazy.

Another scratch to add to the wounds.

It stung.

She struggled on and trips to Moorfields became part of life. They blasted her retinas with thousands of laser shots to try to stop the bleeding. Having her baby had sacrificed her sight.

And she carried on. She would not let the pain and struggles stop her. Her little girl was the only thing that mattered.

As her child grew she taught her to love unconditionally. Personal circumstance with divorce and being called 'hypochondriac' time and time again added strength amongst the tears. Her little one knew how to read and write at the age of three with her by her side.

They sat on the small boxes around the book-filled holders and shelves in the library. They read Dr Seuss and created things for Sunday School. Saving old washing-up bottles they turned them into rockets, and egg-boxes became creatures. She made cakes and her girl licked the spooned mixture. Yet, she was always sick too. Infection after infection; anti-biotics and more anti-biotics.

Being inseparable her girl knew how to inject her Mum's insulin by the age of four, fetched glucose tablets and practised dialling for an ambulance on their telephone which had Buzby on top.

She began to make soft toys for Moorfields as a thank you for their efforts. And she made her girl's clothes, uniform and knitted jumpers.

Surviving as a single mother, picking up small bits of work, unaware of any support.

She slowly lost her eyesight as they performed an operation which stopped the bleeding in her right eye. Once, she was a fine artist. What would she do now?

Carrying on, she persevered, instilling her stubborn determination into her child and giving her strength, for life.

2 yrs 4mths

So Blind

It was a shock.

A new baby, the one she had always wanted, yet she was thrust into grief. Her eyesight wouldn't allow her to see her little girl properly. It was cruel.

It was a struggle.

Deceit.

Blackness and blurriness mixed with flashes and dots.

Before becoming pregnant she had just started her own career of commission work with her fine artwork. Pain had ensured she could not travel far on her moped and she had tried working in an engineering firm as secretary. She had taught herself to type on an old typewriter which now sat upstairs near baby. Then she had successfully applied for a job in the 'path lab', bought a Mini and enjoyed driving.

Now, she found herself unable to work yet alone drive;

those few months before pregnancy were to be her only time. The pain was ever-present and she could not see. Soon after returning home from those long months in hospital she collapsed after being told she was 'lazy' and a 'hypochondriac' as she struggled to feed, sleep, do the housework and cook. All mothers had to endure baby. She was rushed in by ambulance and they helped to stabilise her diabetes. Here she learned that she had severe bleeding on her retinas called 'diabetic retinopathy' and was referred quickly to London to the Moorfields Eye Hospital, the best in the country.

Was it so because this was 'visible' unlike her pain?

Over the years thousands and thousands of laser shots were fired into her eyes. Often her little girl accompanied her with a relative. She relied on her child to guide her through the London Underground as she could not see, with her vision made worse from dilated pupils and laser beams.

Then, her girl stayed home, going to school on the days she went to London. She had to find a phone box with coins used, then later a phone-card to tell her she was on her way back by train. Once she had a near miss at the famous King's Cross escalator fire and it was the time of the IRA bomb scares.

How her girl did worry, all through her childhood and beyond.

When her girl was eight, she was admitted to Moorfields for a vitrectomy. It was the last resort. Laser treatment had stabilised her left eye leaving a small patch of vision in the bottom right of it. Her right eye refused to stop bleeding. So, they replaced the jelly in this eye with an oily substance, making her blind in it but succeeding in stopping the haemorrhage.

She thought about the tears from her child as she came to see her in hospital and then later when she returned home with a patch over her eye.

How to survive?

Time and time again her girl said she should get help. So, together they called Social Services. Now, it was 1989 and her baby was ten years old. With the social worker they completed the Disability Living Allowance forms and were supported. She got a white stick, signed up to the Large Print talking newspaper, had access to the Large Print books from the library and she was able to have a large magnifying glass. For the first time since 1978 she found freedom and independence. She had some money of her own and things started to change.

And throughout all of this time she taught her little girl everything. She sewed, knitted and crafted by touch, making hundreds of soft toys for Moorfields to sell in their hospital shop and her girl joined in. They carted four or five black sacks full every year on the train.

Unfortunately diabetes wasn't finished with just her eyes.

LLL Love Laugh Live

A natural charm oozed from her and a radiant smile of genuine love attracted people. Through her life there had been characterful men. As a young twenty-something she nearly married an Arabian on holiday and spoke fondly of his harem. Together with her best friend that had been an experience as they travelled to Tunisia and Yugoslavia in the days before conflict tore the countries apart.

There was always something to laugh about, a distraction from pain and illness. When you looked at Mum you were drawn into a warmth of cheekiness. She was the epiphany of invisible disability. Without her dark glasses, cane or mobility problems she looked well.

So, let's show something.

You are in severe pain, perhaps you've put your back out or caught your finger in the car door. Ouch! But there is no sign of anything hurting, just your voice to demonstrate. 'You look well,' greets a friend. How do you feel when they say this considering you are screaming inside? Now think of this every day for the rest of your life and you have met the chronic pain of invisible illness. 'Well' can mean more to someone who is unwell, having grieved for their previous abilities and health. Why not say lovely, beautiful or compliment clothes etc instead?

But, Mum chose to hide it, like most of us do, for the sake of a break from dwelling on it.

On her dog walks she met her male friends. She stopped for a chat, flirt and giggle. Sometimes I would find them in the street when I got off the school bus. Then the fish-man asked her to run away with her! She sought my permission, we wanted to stay together, he didn't. So that was that.

One day my friend, I and Mum returned from a dog walk and she found a piece of sponge in the driveway. She prodded it with her stick. As she lifted it the sponge soared through the air, over the hedge and wall and into next door's garden as the dog followed it with her eyes, her head moving comically. We were in fits of laughter and still giggle about it thirty years later.

Then one day I sat on the bathroom stool and air flowed into a rubber glove as I did so raising it like a dead hand. Did I scream and laugh with Mum and my friend!

So, behind the tears, pain and sorrow there was always laughter and love.

That's life. It's called an attitude with gratitude.

It is possible to be happy and be in pain. But, there needs to be a balance of empathy, pain-relief, distraction techniques and love to be able to live and laugh.

Segregation

Alone. She sits curled, knees tucked up and head held down. People pass by and notice nothing. Sobbing into her skirt she dreads the next hour, or two, or three.

Inside her bag is lunch. Sandwiches with cheese spread, an Ambrosia pudding pot and sweet snacks. The same, carefully prepared meal she made the night before. Mum checked but could no longer make it. Later tonight she would go to the garage and get some potatoes from the sack and prepare dinner, and check on Mum, help her wash, change her dressings.

She didn't understand why people didn't love her. She loved them. A sensitive soul with worry on her mind, she was ten years old.

Music meant that some of the other children had a similar interest. But after she made friends they were taken away. Trust, friendship and fun was had, then they were gone. Every year was the same, had been since they moved and met the girl who bullied her, constantly using relational aggression. The passive aggressive ostracism.

But, now, she still loved and remained in touch with her best friend from then. Now, she knew what she had been missing.

Now, she loved herself.

And this fitted with everything in her life. Segregation taught her a lesson. Feminism was held high. Disability was experienced with Mum and now with her. She thought of her Black friends during that time; also segregated. They were blamed for fights, disruption in class, and the girls had to tie their hair back tightly to prevent their natural, beautiful Afro style.

Who was the bully here?

The intersectionality of prejudice, discrimination and abuse crosses paths. But she didn't think any less of herself by supporting her Mum as a child carer now. Then it had been beyond recognition, it was just called love. By thinking Child Carers Matter, Disabled Lives Matter would to her be an equivalent of Black Lives Matter. She thought no less of Black Lives Matter because of her own struggles. And she didn't think All Lives Matter because that's at the top of the stairs. She thought that we have to support all of the different matters first before all lives can even be named. Every single one of us has a cause close to our hearts. Name it. Say it… Matter then consider someone challenging it by saying All Lives Matter, not your cause.

So, she sees a child, in the corner, and thinks, with all of the others to-ing and fro-ing, ignoring her, passing on by, that That Child Matters. Not all of the people in the scene, at this time.

That is where she sees people of colour and Black Lives Matter. Segregated.

She learns about White Privilege. She came from

poverty, abuse, bullying and disability but still takes a step back. Being White means that she doesn't think about colour, unless there is a Black person nearby. She doesn't think White. That is privilege in itself.

Equality will come, she feels sure. But not now. As a Quaker she believes in it and fights for it. Every single person has the light of spirit within them; whether it's God, or something else, it keeps us alive. She chooses to sit with spirit to see where she is led. Ever since she accepted life and followed spirit her life has changed into peace.

Her light is clear, and her dark. She chooses.

Watching the greed and jealousy she learns of the isolation and segregation of the Palestinians with annexation. She listens to the shameful treatment of the Windrush generation. The devastation of our environment has been a battle she has fought since being a child too. She hears fellow Friends saying they are hopeless and don't know what to do.

Her light is clear, and her dark. She chooses.

Please take that decision, to see the light within. Close your eyes, allow thoughts to fade. See the bright, white light inside which is waiting to lead you and listen.

38

Chronic

Witnessing pain in a loved one and not being able to help causes a variety of choices. I chose love as Mum had taught me. Unfortunately that was a sacrifice of the ultimate self-love which I needed. It is only with this recognition that ego becomes lesser and peaceful joy the normal.

From around the age of four I became aware of the seriousness of Mum's diabetes. Having seen hypos with bitten tongue and fainting I knew exactly where the glucose was, how to mix it, how much to add to water and how to dab it onto Mum's lips if she was unconscious. For a hyper I knew how to inject insulin for her. I listened at her door when she went to bed to make sure she was still breathing. And so began the stressful worry which eventually made my own health become worse and worse. Now, quite rightfully, they are linking childhood stress to physical health in adulthood, beyond the blame of anxiety on the mental aspect. Funnily enough it was still after I had settled my anxiety that the label stuck and the exhausting fight to be believed and supported through years of misdiagnosis and blame led to more ill health. This was the same for Mum too.

After her eyesight failed Mum's blood pressure due to kidney damage slowly damaged her kidneys more, which in turn affected her heart, liver and pain. There were countless 24 hour urine sample collections and ferrying of them on the bus to the hospital. I often took time off school to accompany her and guided her past the crowds where her white stick was not noticed by mums with pushchairs. They always took the full brunt of my strong arms as I protected Mum to stop her from being knocked over.

Mum's heart began to struggle more after she had experienced years of breathlessness. Eventually she had stents fitted to battle the plaque of atherosclerosis and I saw her at her very worst in Papworth Hospital. At that point in time she lost her smile but even then gained it back after a small, brief recovery.

As Mum never gave in she always found something else she could do. She felt her way to learn the harp, became abstract in her painting and in her last year took up an Open University course in Ancient Greek!

But, as her feeling in her hands became less and less she was told it was due to knitting. Of course it wasn't. It was the early days when peripheral neuropathy was little understood but eventually this diagnosis was added to her long list and I watched as more parts of her poor body failed.

The neuropathy didn't stop there. It affected her arms up to her elbows, her feet and legs to the knee and made her doubly incontinent. After infection upon infection she had a permanent supra-pubic catheter fitted. The nerve pain and sensations from neuropathy caused taste disturbance, grip loss, severe pain to hot and cold, muscle weakness, cramps, muscle and joint pain and shakiness.

So we made 2004 the best. Mum was waiting for her first dialysis as her kidney function had decreased so much. A fistula was due to be fitted in her arm. It was the most terrifying thing she could think of and she didn't want it.

With some persuading I encouraged Mum to use a wheelchair as she was so stubborn that she would walk everywhere with her delta frame that we didn't make it past the car before she was exhausted. It enabled us to go further, beyond the car, into a lovely garden centre where she could then have an enjoyable walk before she needed it again.

Osteoarthritis in her back, neck and hips was added. Then the treatment for her kidneys caused a new symptom and she started having seizures and TIAs aged

55. With the medication for these liver damage occurred, never to recover.

But what does physical pain and debilitation really mean and do?

Mum was adamant that any dementia would be worse than all she endured. Until the very end she held on to her ability to think her way through life and use the loving peace she held so well to help her and others.

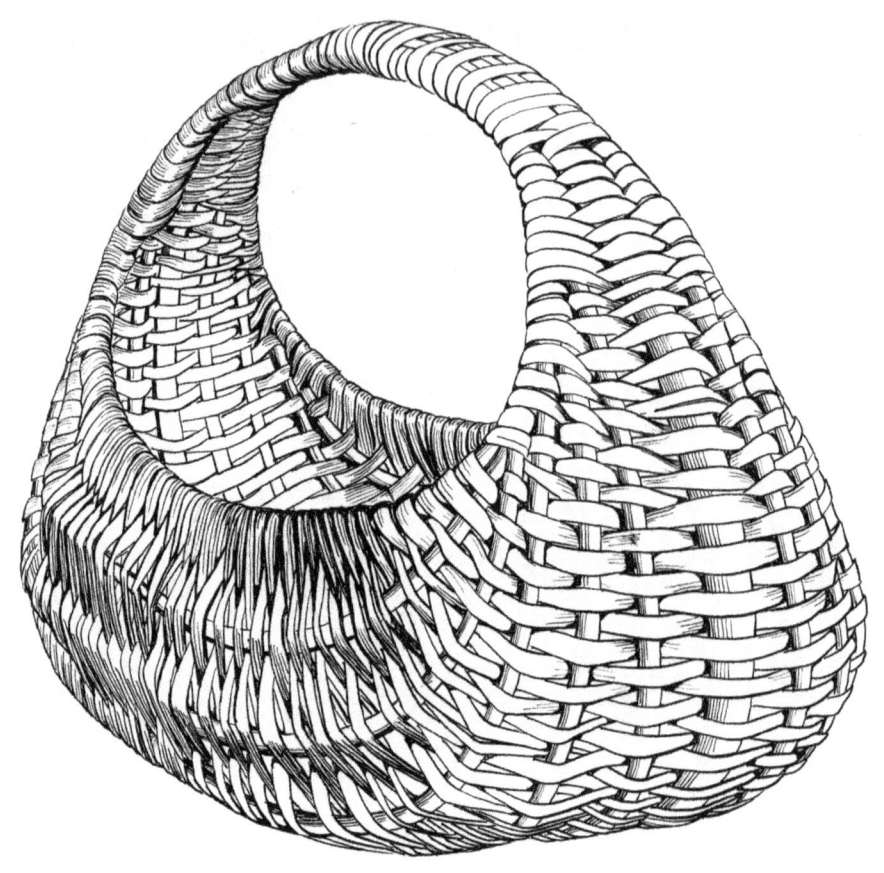

44

Ignorant

They are ignorant, just ignore them.

The response to any difficulty.

To a bully, or bullies. Even pain, health.

Unfortunately no help to a child. A cry of desperation from a loving Mum who was herself isolated and bullied.

There is no blame. It is very difficult to understand unless you were there. The other true guidance Mum felt so much was forgiveness. Is this 'To forgive and forget?'

No.

Forgiveness only comes after healing. Finding peace. Then, it is more complicated. Do I forgive those who are most cruel? Is blame taken away from acts of evil?

No.

The bigger picture is seen and suddenly those two words, ignorance and forgiveness, mutually affect. My response as a child was that ignorance meant you didn't know.

What it really is, is unawareness. A decision wrongly made. We all choose. Only a child cannot through innocence. As a child we are truly unaware. Adulthood brings pathways and awakening. But some do not stop sleeping.

We see success.

As ego leads us to compare, success in others overwhelms our sensitivity and envy kicks in. Their success is our failure. Our failure denotes unfairness. Where does this originate? Attention-driven satisfaction in the shallowness of ego. Strive deeper, don't judge, don't compare. Be happy for them through love. Then you will find peace and love yourself.

Ego is not self-love. The awareness of the light within brings true life and the road to forgiveness.

Mum didn't forgive an evil act. She forgave the person. Guilt and blame grab tightly around the victim even though there is none. It is this we forgive. Wrong choices forgiven. Innocence resurrected and the pure love of spirit heals to peace.

True light brings a child-like happiness where spirit is followed.

Life is accepted and you can shine now.

48

49

Fright or Flight

Once again you stand on the doorstep clutching a small bag. What could she need? She looked out onto the street. Dare she? She was little, no more than six years old. That was the first time.

Even then a homeless existence pulled ever more closer. When she was a little older the police came to school to talk and she saw the alcohol and drugs. But what about the lives of the homeless people? They all had lives. Different lives. They had made a choice of flight. Fighting fright or flight.

The alternative was fright.

A continuous existence of walking on egg-shells. Never knowing what the next minute would bring.

Cold, wet nights on doorsteps. Huddled in gutters and urine-stained clothes wrapped around. It was common to see homeless people. One guy was resident on a bench in the park. Sodden cardboard made another shelter in a shop doorway. People walked on by. Nobody gave money to fuel their addictions. And so, nothing was given.

She was around nine years old then.

There was disgust and apprehension in the crowds of oblivion. Packed like ants marching and marching and marching their heads bowed down.

Why didn't they look up?

She never understood.

And so, time and time again, she stood on her doorstep. A limbo between flight or fright. It lasted for what seemed like forever, childhood seemed to take more time than adulthood and days got faster and faster. Her belief staid her decision. To give up would be to defy God and with prayers every night she could not break a bond of love for Mum. So she stayed and fright or flight was internalised to be physically materialised into a world much later where stress was a proven provocation.

53

Energy

Six long months. The hospital became a home from home. Washing, dressing, liaising, advocating, fighting and loving. Mum had a mild heart attack in January 2005 but then a series of TIAs regularly. Three times she went home. Three times she was rushed back in under the familiar blue lights the very next day.

I spoke to her on the Friday night the last time. She managed a month at home for her final wish. Then on the Saturday she fell unconscious and went straight to ICU.

She waited. We had spoken about death. It was a rare relief knowing exactly what her wishes were and in this time I knew. An unspoken instinct. Calm. Peace.

A brief break, perhaps home for something to eat? No! I was adamant I wanted to stay. And so it was as she died within minutes.

Watching her blood pressure drop. The machine beeps. Slower and slower.

I stroke her arm. 'It's OK sweetheart, don't be frightened, let it go now,' and she dies. I close her eyes.

Years later I watch my partner die. He rips the IV line out, blood spurting everywhere. His oxygen levels are so low, confusion avails and then the morphine, calming, a reassuring presence of relaxation. The same, peaceful expression as life leaves.

Where do you go when that last bit of energy leaves you? Waiting until the end. Peace. A secret listening.

Peace, Forgiveness and Faith

Grief brought wails of emotion and tears, so many tears. Yet being there, watching Mum die also brought an honourable witnessing. It grasped my very being, wrapping my stomach in knots and claiming my appetite.

Throughout my twenty-six years with Mum I grappled with her almost genius quality. So strong was her faith and belief in forgiveness. Never, did I think I would finally understand.

What happens when you do?

Life becomes easier and expectation gives way to acceptance. Every day becomes a bonus and one of unknown opportunity. For many years I meditated, grew my soul, drenched my childhood depression and anxiety with positivity. It worked.

But, it also created a mask of smiles to confront the world. I learned that my peers, colleagues, friends, family were not interested in truth and honesty. They wanted a cover to be drawn over everything with a pretence of happiness. You cannot reach genuine love and joy like this.

Only by facing issues and accepting wrongs can you move on.

The boxes in my head can open as I please and be slammed shut. They should not be filed away to be forgotten and shelved. They lurk in the background, nibbling at you, pulling you further into darkness. I had to find the strength to open them all, in order to close them at will.

So, what about faith?

Is it God?

People are convinced that God would not make us suffer. But, it is our choices, our experience and how we choose to love which brings peace. God is the light within each one of us and to sit still, bathing in this divinity truly gives and enables us to return the gift. I truly believe that a liberating God allows us freedom and our own choices with this bring our experience.

What happens when you do find peace?

You are there for others and no longer afraid. Kindness and love prevail.

Full Circle

Being a child carer brings a lifelong appreciation of love. My mum was vulnerable and isolated; so was I, but it was our world. We both didn't know any better. It was love which got us through such pain and difficulty. There are lots of 'what ifs' but life isn't a regrettable one for looking back on.

As a child I saw my mum as my responsibility as I watched her in so much pain. The downside of this was that I didn't matter, at all.

It has taken me a long time to accept myself as my own person. Now, I have found such peace. It is unbelievable how the challenges have come to make me into the woman I am and how life has literally come full circle.

Self-love was a completely unacceptable and sinful idea in childhood. It meant selfishness and this led to arrogance. I used to think *I can never be arrogant.* Of course

I couldn't be. But, self-love is the opposite of arrogance. I love myself because I have God within me and I am made from his love.

It isn't only about God though. It's because of me. This life I have been given deserves to be loved and cherished. Only by loving yourself can you love others. When you grow up hoping for a cure and relief for the person who is meant to be your caregiver it brings you great empathy. I can honestly say I have never felt jealousy because of this. I wish everyone well. Why? Because I chose to look after Mum. I chose not to run away. There was a strong bond of love and protection between us which somehow sustained all.

Being at peace and finding forgiveness brings wholeness. Yet we think we have done something wrong to need to find forgiveness. We don't only feel guilt because of our wrong-doing. We feel guilty if we have been wronged. *What could I have done to prevent this? Why did he do that to me? Why is Mum in so much pain? What have I done?* This is the complicated affair of self-blame which goes hand-in-hand with a difficulty. By forgiving ourselves we let it go, we don't allow the 'act' or 'circumstance' to be 'right', we just let it be free of us. We lose the ego in the most beautiful way.

A simple, quiet stillness and meditative quality is in my life now. Every day I live each moment. There is a lot of pain, I have an incurable, progressive disease and yet my dreams have come true. And here they are, as an author, being written down and I thank you.

65

Writing by Kathleen

I see a distant haze
And a gently moving sky
I never see the ground below
Only things on high.
I envisage in each passing breeze
A soothing, whispering form
Which always lives for laughter
And rides above the storm.
Of rushing, driving tempests,
Never descending fast.
I'd love to live in this form
With quietude to last.
This space of time I share
With living, never striving,
Fearing, hoping but loving
With a meaning, surviving
Without dreaming.

Many are needed to make up a community which is varied to satisfy each individual.

This community is such a rarity that you never find and never will find peace to give satisfaction to those who wish it as there are in equality those who do not wish it.

There will never be a world to satisfy all.

Inquisity

A child's mind never rests
Always wanting to know why
Bees make hives, birds' nests,
People live, and people die.
Life is that way my little one,
You'll discover more and then
You think again when you're alone
Why am I here?
Too often there is no answer
No one knows why or can tell.
Take the world as you see it
For many are as intrigued as you.
One day the light will shine on you
And tell you why these things are so
Until then, do not wonder
But keep asking 'til you know.

About the Author

Amanda Jones is an author based in beautiful Devon. She has been writing since she was a child and her work includes Historical Fiction, Poetry, Non-Fiction and Short Stories. She is disabled and she has been writing all of her life having both self-published and published work. CaféLit, an online magazine by Gill James, is where many of her short stories, both fiction and non-fiction can be found. Writing is Amanda's lifelong dream and she actively encourages others to follow theirs.

Being a Quaker, Amanda runs the Quaker Arts Network Creative Writing Group and contributes to a blog writing group for Discovering Quakers.

Please join Amanda online through her social media channels:

Amazon
www.amazon.com/author/amandababer

Facebook
www.facebook.com/amandababerauthor

Instagram
www.instagram.com/amanda_jones_aka_baber_author

Instagram
www.instagram.com/missydogbooks/

CafeLit
https://cafelit.co.uk/index.php/meet-our-authors?view=article&id=114:amanda-baber&catid=2:uncategorised

Facebook
https://m.facebook.com/MissysMatters/

Instagram
www.instagram.com/missysmatters/

X
https://mobile.twitter.com/Missysmatters

Pinterest
https://uk.pinterest.com/missysmatters/pins/

YouTube
www.youtube.com/channel/UCrqE6dmZJ3TXpsojksu2BFQ

Please Leave a Review

Reviews are so important to writers. Please take the time to review this book. A couple of lines is fine.

Reviews help the book to become more visible to buyers. Retailers will promote books with multiple reviews.

This in turn helps us to sell more books… And then we can afford to publish more books like this one.

Leaving a review is very easy.

Go to https://amzn.to/4aaud7z, scroll down the left-hand side of the Amazon page and click on the "Write a customer review" button.

Other Books by Amanda Jones

Through her Missy Dog Books Amanda supports good causes, with her first book *Missy and the Whitts* benefitting Charmouth Local History Society. Missy was Amanda's flat-coated retriever and through Missy's dreams we travel back into real history as her adventures are brought to life. She meets real people, real creatures and experiences the past in her sleep. In her waking moments she shares her real life exploits and we meet people on her travels; it might be someone you know. Amanda has illustrated this book too.

The second book in the series is *Missy and the Old Fossils*. Amanda has published this book, chapter by chapter, online on her website on her blog at https://amandababerauthor.wordpress.com/2018/11/06/missy-and-the-old-fossils-intro/

Having a flair for the quirky Amanda also enjoys

writing horror and humorous stories. Her CaféLit stories can be found here: https://cafelitcreativecafe.blogspot.com/search/label/Amanda%20Jones

The Doll's House of Horror can be purchased from her along with *Croc-a-beest*, also illustrated by Amanda. *Missy and the Whitts* can also be purchased through Amazon on Kindle or by contacting her through her website. http://amandababerauthor.wordpress.com/.

Other Publications by Bridge House

Invisible on Thursdays
by Peppy Barlow

INVISIBLE ON THURSDAYS
an esoteric journey

Peppy Barlow

Peppy Barlow is a playwright and screen writer who lives her life looking for meaning and material in all her experiences. In this book she and her friend Persephone/Lucia explore childhood memories - both good and bad - and travel with their children to Crete where ancient myths emerge to haunt them.

A very personal account of a friendship which takes Peppy back to England and ends with Persephone returning to the Underworld. Authentic, brave, honest, funny and touching - the author's voice shines out from these pages.

Author Peppy Barlow guides us through her turbulent and rich life adventures. Truly a life well-lived.

"I loved it… what a roller coaster ride. Living life as it occurred. For me there were laughter and tears in equal measure." (Amazon)

Order from Amazon:

Paperback: ISBN 978-1-914199-16-5
eBook: ISBN 978-1-914199-17-2

Dry River
by Alicia J Rouverol

Sara Greystone's career as a public defender is spiraling after a disastrous court case, and now her husband's IT career is also in jeopardy. A move to California is supposed to get them both back on their feet, but the state is in the midst of a crippling economic downturn- and then Sara's mother falls seriously ill. In the face of migration, illness, unemployment, and the tantalising possibility of infidelity, Sara has to work out who she is and what she really wants.

Spanning 1997 to 2012, *Dry River* echoes Wallace Stegner's classic Angle of Repose, moving across place and time to chart the slow collapse of a marriage alongside a declining US economy.

"Beautifully written story of life's crossroads" (Amazon)

Order from Amazon:

Paperback: ISBN 978-1-914199-44-8
eBook: ISBN 978-1-914199-45-5

www.ingramcontent.com/pod-product-compliance
Lightning Source LLC
Chambersburg PA
CBHW080810120626
46556CB00009B/3281